How Do You Know It's Winter?

By Allan Fowler

Consultants:
Robert L. Hillerich, Ph.D., Bowling Green
State University, Bowling Green, Ohio

Mary Nalbandian, Director of Science,
Chicago Public Schools, Chicago, Illinois

Fay Robinson, Child Development Specialist

CHILDRENS PRESS®
CHICAGO

Series cover design by Sara Shelton

Library of Congress Cataloging-in-Publication Data

Fowler, Allan.
 How do you know it's winter? / by Allan Fowler.
  p. cm. — (Rookie read-about science)
 Summary: A simple description of the characteristics of winter.
 ISBN 0-516-44915-X
 1. Winter—Juvenile literature. [1.Winter.] I. Title.
 II. Series: Fowler, Allan. Rookie read-about science.
QB637.8.F69 1991
508—dc20   91-3129
                                                          CIP
                                                           AC

Printed in China
25 26 27 28 R 12 11   62

How do you know
it's winter?

When falling snow turns the world white, winter has surely come!

Only in winter can you
skate on a frozen pond...

or zip down a hill on
a sled...

or build a funny snowman...

or play in the snow!

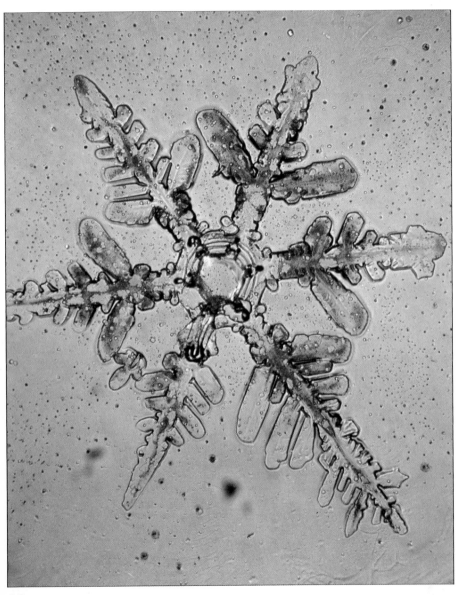

10

Snow is made up of tiny flakes.

And no two snowflakes look alike!

How can you tell it's winter
when there isn't any snow?

If leaves are gone from
the trees...

if the cold, cold air makes
you shiver and you bundle
up to keep warm...

15

if it's already dark outside
when you eat your supper,
then you know it's
wintertime!

Animals covered with fur
don't mind the cold.

But bears and raccoons
sleep through most of the
winter.

Many people celebrate special holidays in winter.

Some people celebrate Christmas.

Families gather around the tree.

Some people celebrate Hanukkah.

Families light candles for
eight days in a row.

In some parts of the world,
it's cold and snowy all
the time.

But in other parts of the world, it's so warm in winter that boys and girls there have never seen snow.

Winter snow is lots of fun to play in.

But aren't you glad that someday the snow will melt, and spring will come back again?

Words You Know

winter

snow

snowflake

snowman

cold

Christmas

Hanukkah

sled
sledding

skate
skating

31

Index

air, 14
animals, 18
bears, 19
candles, 23
Christmas, 20, 31
cold, 14, 18, 24, 30
dark, 16
families, 21, 23
fur, 18
Hanukkah, 22, 31
hills, 7
holidays, 20
leaves, 13
melt, 29
raccoons, 19

skate, 6, 31
skating, 31
sled, 7, 31
sleep, 19
snow, 4, 9, 11, 12, 24, 26, 29, 30
snowflake, 11, 30
snowman, 8, 30
spring, 29
supper, 16
trees, 13, 21
warm, 14, 26
winter, 3, 4, 6, 12, 19, 20, 26, 29, 30
wintertime, 16

About the Author

Allan Fowler is a free-lance writer with a background in advertising. Born in New York, he lives in Chicago now and enjoys traveling.

Photo Credits

PhotoEdit—© Myrleen Ferguson, 21; © Robert Brenner, 23, 31 (top right); © Stephen McBrady, 31 (top left)

Valan—© Kennon Cooke, Cover, 5, 9, 19; © Francis Lépine, 6, 31 (bottom right); © Michel Bourque, 7, 13, 31 (bottom left); © V. Wilkinson, 8; © Harold Green, 10, 30 (top right); © Murray O'Neill, 18; © Fred Bruemmer, 25, 30 (bottom right); © Pierre Kohler, 27; © John Fowler, 28; © Michel Julien, 30 (top left)

© Jim Whitmer—15, 17, 30 (bottom left)

COVER: Grand Tetons, Wyoming